POEMS

OF

CONFORMITY

BY

CHARLES WILLIAMS

the apocryphile press
BERKELEY, CA
www.apocryphile.org

apocryphile press
BERKELEY, CA

Apocryphile Press
1700 Shattuck Ave #81
Berkeley, CA 94709
www.apocryphile.org

First published by Oxford University Press, 1917.
First Apocryphile edition, 2007.

ISBN 1-933993-33-2

TO MICHAL

' Who is she that looketh forth as the morning,
fair as the moon, clear as the sun,
terrible as an army with
banners ? '

CONTENTS

(5)

Contents

The Clerk *and the third* Epiphany *poem have appeared in the* Herald ; Proserpina *in the* Saturday Review. *I am indebted to the Editors for permission to reprint them here.*—C. W.

Proserpina

Now our love returns at last,
  For the secret months are spent!
She hath laid aside her vast
  Majesty of government.
  Mother, now thy child is found!
O! we can but look aghast:
  Heart and tongue alike are bound.

Proserpina, O was this,
  This the loveliness we saw
Or hath royalty in Dis
  Girded thee about with awe?
  Did this grave and fateful voice,
These thy regnant hands of law,
  Ever in our games rejoice?

Goddess' child indeed thou art,
  And thy mother now no more
Presseth thee against her heart
  As at morning heretofore:
  Courtesy she yieldeth, such
As her sisters, on their part,
  Grant thee, without smile or touch.

'Sister' cried our lips of old;
  'Sister' saith thy mother now,
While our frighted eyes behold
  Deity upon thy brow.

Proserpina

Lo, we yield thee head and knee !
Was our greeting overbold
 That so often pleasured thee ?

As in Enna's fields thou wert
 Shalt thou never be again ;
When the trodden flowers' hurt
 Smote thee with thy heaviest pain.
 Thou hast seen the Eternal Lord
Measuring unto men desert,
 And thy spirit hath adored.

O for her who with us trod,
 Loving day and sunlight, whom,
Yielding service to her nod,
 Loved we, ere thy voice was doom
 And thy vision destiny ;
Ere the presence of a god
 Mightily o'ershadowed thee.

Troy

I. ANDROMACHE

In Ilion fifty towers are set, whereof
   Hector, that strongest, who is set to be
   A warning and a terror toward the sea,
Is glad at heart on this day's dawn for love :
To whom with music through the temples move
   Feet of a maiden, maiden-circled, she
   Whose name being called of men Andromache
Gleams like white Pergamos all peers' names above.

Troy many-palaced, single-lorded Troy,
   Virgin like Pallas' spear to Pallas' grip,
    Like Aphrodite land-poised from the tide,
Joyous and crownèd city, this new joy
   By Hector's hand crowns and by Priam's lip
    Salutes, and as in bridal hails the bride.

II. HELEN

Not thee alone, Helen, did thy new lord
   Through that long night in thy Greek palace woo,
   But his own native city's false hands drew
In thine from law, broke in thy troth her word :
Wherefore she knows thee now and does accord
   To thee full honour, swears herself anew
   Thine and thy leman's lover, brings thereto
Skill of war-chariot, cunning of the sword.

Ascend upon the walls, Helen, and look,
   Companioned by the young Andromache,
Thither where, far beyond Scamander's brook,
   The lawless, lustful, fierce barbarians dwell :
Turn thyself then, gaze northward, canst thou tell
   How far off is that line of shore, that sea ?

Troy

III. HECUBA

DIDST thou grow old, Troy, as thy queen grew old,
  Honoured in sons, rich in kings' amity,
  Lady of households, till there came to thee
Argos and Ithaca with commandment cold?
Whose faces ever now thy dreams behold
  Storm through thy walls with shouts to victory,
  Whom each new morn dreads lest that morn should see
Such end as thy mad daughter hath foretold.

Shall Helen comfort thee at all, O queen?
Or shall her beauty willingly be seen
  For whose old lord's sake each new fight is won?
Or her voice break the echo heard in thee
Of Priam's feet before thy gate when he
  Bore Hector home, in guard of Thetis' son?

IV. CASSANDRA

QUEEN Hecuba is dead and no more known;
  The slave Andromache by Pyrrhus' chair
  Waits; only now still by a royal stair
The feet of Helen mount her royal throne:
Whose eyes, whose mouth have mocked thy sight, thy moan,
  How oft, Cassandra! since in thy despair
  Were none sure-hearted through Troy's bounds to share,
Save some few old men, blind, morose, alone.

O Troy, whose name was once Andromache,
  Helen, while wantonly thou didst rejoice,
    Hecuba, ere thou yet hadst ceased to reign,
    What shalt thou be more than a cry of pain
  Hereafter through the nations, than the voice
Of a prophetess in her adversity? ·

At Dawn

It is fallen ! it is fallen !   Militant
  Hell all the heights of heaven ramparted
  Hath ta'en : the ruin of them goes up in fire.
Rejoice, O Lucifer ! be jubilant,
  Lords of the Pit ! ye have what ye desire.
Your storm hath rent the New Jerusalem
As a man's fingers tear his garment's hem :
  And whither is the Maker of it fled ?

It is fallen ! it is fallen ! Michael's sword
  Is broken and Ithuriel's spear.   Alone
  In that dire rout the high prince Azrael
Scarce holds the River of Life, and by its ford
  Stays the victorious pursuit of hell.
The meadows of the Lamb are no more sweet
To pasture : they are pressed with burning feet,
  And by hot winds the crystal sea is blown.

It is fallen ! it is fallen !   All the stars
  Whisper to one another, and the night
  Escapes in terror from this fearful East.
Moon upon moon makes sure each gate with bars,
  Sun upon sun.   Creation from its least
World to its mightiest darkens all its towers,
And leaves its walls unkept of any powers,
  Lest one last Fugitive should come in sight.

At Dawn

It is fallen ! it is fallen ! If He speed
   To find some refuge through His universe,
   What place shall open to Him ? Shall the day,
Shall darkness, to His urgency give heed?
   Or time and space have rest for His array?
Lo ! whatsoever sphere shall dare protect
Or shelter that long flight, let it expect
   The noise of His pursuer, and the curse.

It is fallen ! it is fallen ! yea, but, Earth,
   What wind now shakes thee ? to make Whom secure
   Dost thou, laborious, build thy cloud on high?
Call out thy succours, call on pain and mirth,
   Winter and spring : thou shalt not Him deny.
The City of God is fallen, but in thee,
O blessèd Earth, gathers His potency,
   Thou art His hiding-place : thou shalt endure.

Ballade of Building

AELSWITH who built to the praise of Her
　　Whose glory is most plain,
Walkelyn who founded Winchester
　　To all men's after gain,
　　Builders of Sarum, of Romsey fane,
Princes and priests long gone,
　　Knew all that more than this was vain,—
' One stone on another stone.'

Bishop or queen, each labourer
　　Builded in half disdain ;
' What good', they said, ' though our word make stir
　　Trowel and hod and crane ?
　　For this at best shall the work remain,
To teach one thing alone,—
　　The marvel and might that sets with strain
One stone on another stone.'

It is told of the days when great deeds were
　　That there was a king in Spain
Planned a church for his sepulchre ;
　　'Mid pomp of his whole demesne
　　The second brick to the first was ta'en :
Then he ceased and from his throne
　　Cried : ' Lo, be this the word of a reign,
One stone on another stone.'

B　　　　　　　(13)

Ballade of Building

Prince, dig and build and set in train
  Works, that thy name be known :
But only, at ending, of this be fain,
  One stone on another stone !

Ballade of a Street Door

As I came up into the town
  Wherein my father's house abide,
I met a man in tattered gown,
  In ragged garment blowing wide,
  With terror fleet and open-eyed ;
' Ho, whither now so fast, I pray ? '
  Fearfully looked he back and cried :
' I pulled the bell and ran away !

' Good sir, if thou hast held renown
  Among this people, be my guide !
I from their welcome, not their frown,
  In shelter would obscurely hide.
  For when, being tired, a latch I tried,
Whence came a sound of revels gay,
  Fear rose within me like a tide,—
I pulled the bell and ran away.

' A voice called " Bring the festal crown ! "
  And running footsteps gateward hied,
Wherethrough I heard, as they came down,
  Great names that challenged and replied,
  And torchlight through the chinks I spied :
My soul became a wild dismay,
  And as the doors began to slide
I pulled the bell and ran away ! '

L'Envoi

Prince, was it you and I whose pride
  So turned, so fled, upon our Day ?
Was it our voices then which sighed
  ' I pulled the bell and ran away ' ?

Ballade of Numbers

BEFORE the dawn of the first of days
  Ere yet in the heaven the sun grew bright
Over this earth and its devious ways,
  And around us the planetary might
  Swung to the order of its flight,—
Ere the earth was made or the worlds begun
  The finger of God began to write :
'Three times seven are twenty-one.'

High are the poets and high their praise ;
  In the darkness of ages they hold the light ;
In fear and honour and deep amaze
  They keep the treasures of life aright.
  The makers of song in all men's sight
Weave music, but soon their web is spun
  If they know not of this thing the depth and height,—
'Three times seven are twenty-one.'

Kings whom a trembling world obeys,
  Heroes in ancient armour dight,—
All these shall pass with their great arrays,
  Lords of council and lords of fight,
  Roman and Greek and Ishmaelite ;—
Yet this shall remain when all is done,
  For to this the Maker of things is plight :
' Three times seven are twenty-one.'

L'ENVOI
Prince, on our road comes down the night,
  Long is the race and hardly run :
Still hold we sure in a world's despite
  ' Three times seven are twenty-one.'

The Clerk

THE clerk sat on a stool
   And added up a column,
Looking a very fool,
   Staid he was and solemn.
He said : 'Nineteen and one,
   Mark nought and carry two,'
And that was all that he had done
   And all that he could do.

The clerk sat on his stool
   And another line began :
The heroes called him fool
   But God had called him man.
He said : 'Two fives are ten
   And carry one along.'
The devil shuddered in his den
   And Heaven broke forth in song.

Richmond Park

THREE men came over Richmond Park,
  In friendly jocund mood ;
The wind blew dusk, the wind blew dark ;
  Great trees about them stood,
Those on the right were drowned in mist,
  To the left they grew a wood.

There was a friend to right of me,
  There was a friend to left.
My soul was 'ware, all suddenly,
  It trod a dangerous cleft.
My heart between two strange hearts beat,
  Of livelihood bereft.

I knew not either alien heart,
  Nor either alien tone,
Nor what from ambush there would start ;
  Softly they walked unknown.
I dropped to separating depths,
  And drifted there alone.

But God drew back this soul of mine
  Into its earthly ark ;
I saw the lights of Putney shine
  Beneath us in the dark,
And—God be thanked !—I heard my friends
  Talking in Richmond Park.

Inland Travel

WHEN all our fellowship were young,
  We took a task in hand,
And west away from London
  We sought the holy land:
    The high land, the deep land,
      The land that none can see,
    The dolorous land of Logres,
      The coasts of Christentie.

Intelligence came round us
  In tavern, school, and kirk,
And west away through England
  We sought the holy work:
    The high work, the long work,
      The work that none can see,
    The work that first of adepts wrought
      And called it Christentie.

The North Sea and the Channel
  Bring mighty ships to wreck,
But the west seas beat for ever
  On the rock of Carbonek:
    The high rock, the lone rock,
      The rock that none can see,
    The rock that men call Cephas
      In tongues of Christentie.

Conformity

MAID's love that kinship holds in it
To all loves known of mortal wit,
  Beneath the ageing stars,
Being a mother and a chief,
An indefectible belief,
  Blinded by joyous wars,

Hath, sealed in ease of comeliness,
Friendship, than all things else no less.
  Thou know'st, ah *belle amie*,
How dear beyond all amorous grace
The ceremonial embrace
  Pledging that amity.

Thou know'st; but O thou know'st how still
The burning master of our will
  ˏ A single thought transcends,
Illumining with unity
The million manifests of thee,
  Beginnings, centres, ends.

Alien perfections in thee find
A secret reconciling Mind;
  But O how each hath kept
Distinguishable subtlety,
And is in his own mystery
  Himself the sole adept.

Conformity

What cunning hours are pledged, O Song,
Of privy meditations long
   To thy directer sway!
Nor her imperial head withdrew
Your right prerogatives from you,
   Companions of my way!

Affection unto each recurs
In regular obedience ; hers
   The fertile words that heal,
The sacred choriambics are,
But yours the chief odes secular,
   The laws, the Commonweal.

Yours,—by the thousand nights we knew
When the day's tedium broke, with you
   To explore and to dispute,
When laughter, deeper than delight,
Shook with the wind of mental height
   Where very selves salute.

O rooms and roads of gay contest,
Journey and argument and jest,
   From Kew to Harpenden!
Where, while the days made man of me,
My love felt yours amazedly,—
   Men splendid among men.

Yours,—by one admiration more
Than all such old fields reckoned o'er
   Of intellectual storm,
One marvel, that, while fears are rife
Amid men's hearts, your lives to Life
   So mightily conform.

Conformity

Since first, upon his mother's breast,
A single *credo* each professed
   With no dissenting breath,
Till we to that convention come
Where all remonstrances are dumb
   And men conform to death,

You through insult, O dear and strong,
Of ghostly or material wrong,
   Through bitterness that mocks,
Turn not, nor falter, nor recede,
From aught of sacrificial need,
   Vitally orthodox!

Spring and the poets and the hills,—
No joy but voice of yours fulfils
   And makes more great in me;
No pain but your obedience bore;
No cowardice but fails before
   Your holy mockery!

If from one hesitating heart
Honour for that courageous part,
   For spur, ensample, lure,
Of deed or doctrine, be of worth,
You master craftsmen of the earth,
   Be of that honour sure!

Honour to all,—but first to you
For danger's sake in love be, who
   With love and danger glow
Where now, the sword upon her loins,
An England praised of Milton joins
   The France that learned Rousseau,

Conformity

Where now men see, to her old wars,
And breaking kings and dukes and tsars,
  The Revolution come,
Where they whose high plots bore her down
Look and lament, deny or crown,
  The Belgian martyrdom.

(Of you, in Surrey, yet ere blood
Parted for ever mood from mood,
  The tryst was kept with two:
O that last way, as war shut down,
From Dorking pines to Guildford town,
  Of night and dawn and you!)

For the blood's peril first be you
Named, by a mind which not else knew
  Degree, that friendship wrongs:
But, binding loved name to loved name,
Gathers them all—with what of shame!—
  In these remindful songs!

What else to render back for all
You gave and give,—while thoughts recall
  How each heart condescends!
One moment let a weak tongue praise
Your lofty, your excelling ways,
  O kings of me, my friends!

Emigravit

MORTAL, of mortals hardly Earth
Knew love or laughter more of worth ;
Immortal, join the immortals, find
Laughter nor love thou left'st behind.

May 20*th*, 1915

BEATING heart and climbing brain,
   Roaming foot and searching tongue,
Get no more of loss or gain,
   For the soul hath gone along.

Now of all fine things on earth,
   Tales and tastes and towns to see,
Less of wealth hath less of worth
   For our double poverty.

In a beggared lane we go,
   Palsied of the better hand ;
Purposes none else can show
   Are for ever hidden land.

O the songs we shall not sing !
   O the deeds we shall not do !
O the robbed hours that shall bring
   In your thought's place thought of you !

Now the past is robbed also ;
   You, being gone from us and all,
With the ghostly years shall grow
   Fainter and phantasmical.

And of us inconstant, you
   Shall have like inconstant mind,
In so many ventures new
   Slipping us you leave behind,—

May 20th, 1915

With the town which you espied,
 Where it yet on earth shall be,
Built about you on each side,
 The Republic's liberty;

As you saw her, rising far
 To the great design of man,
As you heard her to her war
 Call by ban and arrière-ban;

As your pledges you redeemed,
 Serious and gay unthrift,
To the politic you schemed:
 All magnificent in gift!

Only once, if aught awake
 Still in you of death or pain,
For our loving's ancient sake,
 O remember me again!

O courageous, new in power,
 Heavened afar from earth and me,
In my own departing hour
 Knit again our federacy!

Hope

WHEN we were lost in the night
  Down grass-paths old,
Miserable, without light,
  Hungry and cold,
Then your voice cried 'Hush!' through the dark.

We saw no lantern nor heard
  Any man near:
But we stood still at the word
  With hope to hear,
For your voice cried 'Hush!' through the dark.

When Satan had hold on me
  To make an end,
In heaven, in earth, I could see
  Sign of no friend:
Then your voice cried 'Hush!' through the dark.

Does one draw near where I grope,
  To put off death?
I see him not, nor have hope,
  Yet hold my breath:
For your voice cried 'Hush!' through the dark.

Endings

KNOCK, knock, and it shall open.
Shall it open?
For it seems that none at all
Hear our call.

Knock, knock, and it shall open.
Did ye try—it may be true,—
Ere ye knocked,
Ere against the door ye beat
With insistent hands and feet,
If by chance it stood unlocked?
If the catch
Were undone, the bolt unshot?
O it may be :—linger not,
Lift the latch,
Hasten through.

Seek, seek, and ye shall find.
Shall we find?
Seeing we so long have sought,
But for naught.

Seek, seek, and ye shall find.
Did ye look and search for truth,
Ere ye went,

Endings

Ere ye rode through countries far
Underneath an arctic star,
Through the town wherein ye spent
Every day ?
What if all these roads were vain
Till ye turn towards it again ?
So it may
Be, in sooth.

Ask, ask, and ye shall have.
Shall we have ?
Often have we come with prayer,
Yet are bare.

Ask, ask, and ye shall have.
Ere ye brought, with faces grave,
As to kings,
High petitions fearfully,
Did ye go not with your plea
Where your father works and sings,
Where ye live ?
Ask of him,—O wise it were !—
Ere of the king's minister.
He can give :
Ask and have.

Song

Scorn not, lovers, Luck your god,
  Many a cold maid he
To her bachelor hath showed,
  Red with angry glee.
Though her 'custom'd brow were bleak,
At a chance, warm grew her cheek.
    Chance, be kind !
    Teach all mays to know their mind.

Luck, when kisses keep no worth
  In a soon-tired tryst,
Makes as soon for Love new worth
  At a time unwist.
Pray we then that every sweet,
At a chance, her lad shall meet.
    Chance, be kind !
    Teach all mays to know their mind.

A Song of Opposites

EACH separate thing, howe'er it be
  By manifold devices known,
Hath in them all a unity,
  And is in all ways that alone.

Perfect the bird in song or flight,
  Perfect the flower in growth or smell ;
So in each separate mental sight
  Perfect my maid's completions dwell.

In many opposites revealed
  She wholly is herself in each,
And does dividual vision yield
  But my dividual sense to teach.

So, as young doves that try the air
  Although her glances timid be,
The heavens themselves shall not outdare
  Her delicate audacity.

So will her mind, in fellowship
  Of art, see, hear, rebuke, admire,
Whose heart, in touch of breast and lip,
  Flames upward in love's flying fire.

She who is glad at vanities
  And laughs in temporal delights
Hath wisdom yet in mysteries
  Which are the dreams of anchorites.

A Song of Opposites

So, visible in many a turn,
  Moves her essential unity,
And sensitively so I learn
  To know the customary she.

O moments that should make me wise !—
  But O the rarer times that be,
When she withdraws from any guise
  To open singularity !

When all her spirit is expressed
  In all her body's holy charms,
And only she is manifest
  Ere yet she leans into my arms !

A Song of Implications

Fire in blood or blood in fire
Shaped the form of my desire ;
Yet, of this fair natural,
What the pure original ?
Clouds the vein-impulsèd skin
O'er arterial light within ?
Or hath here essential blood
A corporeal flame indued ?

In her speech or silence dwells
All, Creation hides or tells ;
Close her hushèd lips behind,
Its communicable Mind ;
While her vainest riot is
Interfused with stillnesses.
Pause in her or utterance
Weds the opposèd circumstance.

Of her body or her ghost
Who knows which is native most ?
My soul to her lordly face
Fac me salvum ever prays ;
Yet my most of earth delights
In her soul's more dainty flights.
Which for wear did th' other don
To bring down salvation ?

A Song of Implications

Thus though I for joy perplex
Still our riddling intellects,
Yet, to find or follow these
Alternate intelligences,
Thought between our lips is dull
Which when dumb are worshipful,
When, dear disputations o'er,
Kissing-dumb, sweet paramour

Marriage

O THINK not, sweet, to what wild end
    Thy love soe'er is bent,
Thou canst that breast of sighs commend
    To more relinquishment,

To fuller licence canst commit
    Than knew'st thou this long while,
Since once the yielding heart of it
    Was flagrant in a smile,

Since once, when truest modesty
    Itself no more mistook,
Thy spirit's passion, shaken free,
    So triumphed in one look,

That never can surrender new
    More openness imply,
And all thou canst for ever do
    Shall that but ratify.

Sonnets

I

As once the sea from dyke-walls loosed in flood
   Drowned or drove wide the standards of Castile,
So fails my thought before this angry blood
   Thy beauties wilder, who taught'st it to feel.
The joyous beacons burning from thy heart
   Shook the calm-skyèd region of my mind,
But O what magic spiritual art
   These nerves and sinews to thy rule assigned ?
Is now my body held for mine no more ?
   Or rather doth a more profounder I,
Which that first I willed never to explore,
   Through flesh and blood go trembling visibly ?
     O rain, these else dry channels thou sett'st free,
     And gleam'st, O sun, on the forth-rushing me !

II

I, Fair,—O dreadful nearness ! O twin sounds
   That sole in such proximity assume
Their pomp of personage, and do the bounds
   Of else but legended citadels illume !
No song in any language save its own
   Hath its own sweetness, nor except in thee
Is even my name to its right honour known,
   And ah, what meaning hast thou but by me ?
Now silent and amazèd rests my mind,
   For where I sought an inn of rhyme, a small
Rude house of speech to rest at, lo, I find
   The spires and temples of the capital.
     This music dumbs its sequence: 'thou and I'
     More words serve nothing but to signify.

Sonnets

III

ASK me again if truth be in my verse,—
　　Which now to prove will I not imprecate
On any falsehood a religious curse,
　　Or hold upon its theme precise debate.
But if I call the spirit of it forth,
　　And do of life dis-soul this mimic sphere,
Compelling from bright south or threat-dark north
　　The Word which bore and breathes in all words here,
Then thine own simulacrum mayst thou see,
　　Whose equal truth let thy true conscience gauge,
And judge thyself thereby : this Mystery
　　Only the dogmata of thee doth stage.
　　　　Part of my song thou dost already prove,
　　　　And shall the rest as thou shalt truly love.

IV

No faery balm of love on eyelids laid
　　But, howsoe'er it shows the immortal thee,
Leaves visible an all-too-mortal maid
　　Apparent in her fault and frailty.
I know her casual, wilful, insolent,
　　With little sloths round high intention curled,
Half-sullen in a half-abandonment,
　　Part scornful, part obsequious, to the world.
That same intolerant disquiet, unused
　　To the new liberty of our large love,
Its law with licence or with greed confused
　　And meant its faith by jealousy to prove.
　　　　Sweet, pardon ! love were yet too blind and dull
　　　　Unless it knew in truth and looked in full.

(37)

Sonnets

V

WHAT other heart attempted, ere I dared,
   The essay of thy magnanimity?
O marvel not if then were favours spared
   From that too-much-divided self of thee!
For then, like green slips, all thy fresh desires
   Pierced forth to winter, urged by heart-felt spring,
Then lonelily o'er many mystic shires
   Seeking its nest thy spirit toiled a-wing;
Then soul and body were with longings stirred
   Which now like miracles are brought to pass:
Thou art come home, come home! the new spring's bird
   Drops to its shelter in the new spring's grass.
      Conscience of heart, conscience of soul, made one;
      And all thyself born into unison!

VI

How many a woman is by process ta'en!
   Of her rich land some robber-prince of men
Raids first the marches, then the sensuous plain
   Seizes, then towers of dream, the throne's self then.
But thou, O islanded from such defeat!
   O thou Atlantis whence all pirates fail!
At once my ragged and disfurnished fleet
   Lett'st all thy crimson navies forth to hail.
Nay, now too humbly thy advance I wrong;
   Thou hadst not why to aspire or condescend;
Nor war nor flight provoked thy love along,
   Equal we wheeled unto an equal end.
      Wiles are for others, we as best behoved,
      Solely and simply each, loved and were loved.

Sonnets

VII

WHEN Absence, as beneath the moon a cloud,
  Love o'er all reach of circumstance distils,
Devotion's convent-walls to thee seem vowed,
  And steep toward thee the pass of labour's hills :
Upon all friendship thou who art no friend,
  Or art by but an accident of grace,
Dost indirectly thy great worth expend,
  And hold'st the least acquaintancy in place.
All friendliness hath reason for its cause
  As born of honour, custom, or delight ;
But thou, unreasonably the fount of laws,
  To thine own harm dost lesser loves incite,
    Such strength springs in them from thy love—O rare !
    That with thyself they vie and would compare.

VIII

WITH the divine Tertullian let's believe
  That faith to things impossible is due—
That other maids, Fair, other loves receive,
  And other lovers have their ladies too.
This sworn for doctrine, none, I vow, we meet,
  But are in love or shall be or have been !
With what an air the meanest fellows greet !
  How reticently runs the maddest quean !
How high, how bright, all strangers' faces seem
  As bound from bridal ! in a single kiss
Civic equality hath all his theme,
  And civic revolution springs from this—
    Civic revolt, till all, from whatso dens,
    For that love's sake are held free citizens.

Sonnets

IX

THE lilies of thy marching oriflamme
    Lead on the leopards of my heart's crusade,
Against the walls of Mahmud or the Cham
    Following thy vibrant voice of escalade.
Too long the world—proud infidel !—hath kept
    Love's place of kisses unto man's much loss ;
Too long Religion dreamed while lovers slept ;—
    Now peers-at-arms all they assume the Cross.
Now in that Zion the Crescent whose thin light
    Is borrowed from our own Song, Sword, and Sun
Before our storm of beauty falls to flight :
    From sacramental joys world's pleasures run.
        Love's central height and all his ways therefrom
        Once more are fallen, are fallen to Christendom.

X

I FOLLOW, follow, down the ways of sense,
    Channels rock-roofed that find the mid o' the world,
Or icy peaks of heavenly virtue, whence
    The whole creation's avalanche was hurled,—
Thou all the journey's end ! In crowds I mix
    Amid the jostled pieties of mankind :
Lo, this new doctrine of the crucifix
    Lies hid in thee and thee in it I find.
I see from heaven the great Republic glide
    And hear on earth her raid against the thrones,
Thy glancing eyes lovers from foes divide,
    Her form in thee my sight, my hearing owns.
        So much thou of all beauty art the sum
        All loves to thee must for their pattern come.

Sonnets

XI

WHEN the first eagles of thy empire shone
  About the tribal priesthood of my mind
By them came law, no new religion ;
  Thine image ruled, but thou remain'dst behind :
Till from the sunrise a great Eagle came
  (Out of the East, O love, the shouting East),
Flying on mighty pinions all aflame
  With words of that celestial Syrian Priest.
'Mid thunder, wars, and tossing towers it ranged,
  Clouding the dawn with wings, yet dropping fire,
O'er my revolting Europe, which it changed
  To Christentie, a land of song and lyre.
    So lightened o'er my path thy face and form,
    A law, a creed, a rapture, and a storm !

XII

I SAW a mighty Spirit, high in worth :
  O dazzling light, O splendour, who art thou ?
' Two lovers were we while we dwelled on earth,
  And endlessly two lovers rise we now.
Translucent glows my body to her soul '—
  ' Like fragrance in his soul my body dwells.
O love, yet this division lasts, my dole ! '
  ' O love, how reach we to Love's Wisdom else ? '
Still serve ye Love, as once on earth ye would ?
  ' Hark, hark, all lovers triumph in the Christ,
In him exult the wedded soul and blood,
  Who, kindling love, hath still for love sufficed !
    And lo, himself '—' O love, no more ; turn, turn !
    Ours not to gaze whereon the Christ's eyes burn.'

(41)

On Pilgrimage

HOWE'ER ye walk disguised who through this land,
   This Sultanate of misbelievers, move
(For only the mad poets, Allah's hand
   Hath smit, dare name the Nazarean Love),

At sunset, while even these Moslemah pray,
   Draw o'er your brows your silence, go apart :
O sojourners, Love's pilgrims, stop and say
   The litanies and credos of your heart !

'There is One God : let faithful men receive
   His law', a voice peals the world's roofs above :
But ye with crossed hands utter, 'I believe
   In love (ah me !), in love (ah, sweet !), in Love.'

In the Land of Juda

WHERE did you meet your love, young man?
　Where did you meet your love?
' I met my love in a noisy room
　With a carven roof above.'

What did you say to your love, young man,
　With all your mother wit?
' " How hot it is ! " or " How do you do? "
　And there was an end of it ! '

Who was beside you then, young man?
　Who was beside you then?
' Gaspar, Melchior, Balthazar,
　And a crowd of shepherd-men ! '

What did you say to them, young man,
　Silently, through the din?
' " Princes, when ye come in to her,
　I pray you, lead me in." '

Gratia Plena

WHEN, an unwitting angel, I
   Assumed the *Ave*, and again
Closed that whole past of prophecy
   Which rules each love's collateral strain,
What word but this hadst thou for me,
Ecce ancilla Domini !

Surely the earlier Gabriel heard
   But a provincial dialect,
Then care not though in thee the word
   Some common accent did affect :
Religion knows thy cry and thee,
Ecce ancilla Domini !

Thy life, that, taught beneath the law,
   Hardly a newer sweetness lacked,
Alert, the approaching heavens saw
   And bound them to fulfil their pact.
Breathless, thou sprang'st to them and me,
Ecce ancilla Domini !

I lose the angel from my sense—
   What angel can with thee compare,
Since, for that swift heart's recompense,
   Himself the god established there?
Yet clasp and cling, O more than me !
Ecce ancilla Domini !

Presentation

WHAT thoughts, what meditations new,
  Since first between our lips, my Fair,
An orison of kisses grew,
  And our clasped hands became a prayer,
Have we, together or alone,
Pondered ! what contemplations known !

What marvels in what mysteries !
  How soon with them began to blend
Reports, hints, glimpses, prophecies,
  And premonitions of an End !
As if the doom that shall destroy
Was ay original in Joy.

Nor less the Simeon of our creed
  With harsh voice threats the thing we know :
'Yea, visibly did Love once bleed ?
  A sword shall pierce your hearts also.
Think ye that Love shall faint to death,
And your love still draw lively breath ? '

What tragic moment in this time,
  In some futurity's new birth,
Shall force us up that hill to climb,
  Shall cloud our Sun and shake our Earth ?
By what desire shall Love be priced
Or in what anger sacrificed ?

D   (45)

Presentation

What lawfulness or lack of law,
    Betrayal (an Apostle fell!),
Us to that Death shall drive or draw?
    Messiah shall thy cunning sell?
Or shall—O dread of dreads!—by me
Love come unto his end in thee?

Perchance he, in this pain of thought,
    This bitter but accepted fear,
Enough of crucifixion wrought
    And works his resurrection!   Dear,
Livelong be our entreaty this,
To feel the sword in every kiss!

Orthodoxy

Now to thy heart thy hand hath caught
    The fingers of mine own,
Thy body's secret doctrines now
    Are felt and proved and known :
More wisdom on thy breast I learn
    Than else upon my knees :
O hark, thine honour ! orthodox,
    Destroyer of heresies !

Too reckless promulgation
    Thy virgin face denies,
Yet my schismatic selfhood fails
    Before thine ardent eyes ;
Thine arms are fast about my neck,—
    Embracing pieties !
O hark, thine honour ! orthodox,
    Destroyer of heresies !

In thee hath Logic brought to end
    Her teaching rational,
Heights of unreasonable faith
    Tower up to thee nor fall ;
Thy person puts to utter trial
    Creeds and theologies :
O hark, thine honour ! orthodox,
    Destroyer of heresies !

Orthodoxy

By storm the heavens are taken,
    Thou by triumphal storm,
Yet only Love's last potence wins
    Thy half-relinquished form ;
All despotisms else go down,
    All shifting anarchies
Thou tramplest under : orthodox,
    Destroyer of heresies !

O new-conceivèd, doubly born,
    Immaculate in love,
As She, that first of Christendoms,
    Deigns later dogmas prove,
So by the kisses of thy mouth
    New laws and sanctities
Teach ! hark, thine honour, orthodox,
    Destroyer of heresies !

Ecclesia Docens

FOUR signs whereby the humblest
   The certain Church may tell,
The learnèd doctors teach us.
   (God send we learn them well !)
One in her thousand aspects,
   And holy as her birth,
Throughout all nations Catholic,
   Of Apostolic worth.
     And lo, in thee, O dear and fair,
      I end awhile my search,
     Believing in the Catholic
     And Apostolic Church.

Thy turmoil and forbearing,
   Thy strong inviolacy,
Thy sorrow, mirth, submission,
   Grow all to unity ;
Through all thy thousand virtues
   That spirit which hath run
Is manifested mightily,
   Within my arms, for one.
     And lo, in thee, O sole and fair,
      Awhile I end my search,
     Believing in the Catholic
     And Apostolic Church.

Ecclesia Docens

Thou lend'st the whole creation
  An awful holiness,
Till all things with new wonders
  Do my affections bless.
Effectual consecrations
  In rumours of thee fly,
Who, sanctified to glory,
  Goest forth to sanctify.
    And lo, in thee, O pure and fair,
    Awhile I end my search,
    Believing in the Catholic
    And Apostolic Church.

Yet mov'st thou in no faction,
  No word sectarian hast,
O type of all men's future,
  And their accorded past !
For still I follow, learning
  Thy individual use,
Quod semper, quod ubique,
  Et quod ab omnibus.
    And lo, in thee, O general fair,
    Awhile I end my search,
    Believing in the Catholic
    And Apostolic Church.

The high Apostles' warfare
  Against the princely North
Thy sudden motion urges,
  Thy temples' gleam shows forth.

Ecclesia Docens

Their sacred dogmas colour
  Thy sacerdotal eyes,
Traditional, pontifical,
  Thy hands, as theirs, are wise.
    And lo, in thee, O priestly fair,
      Awhile I end my search,
    Believing in the Catholic
      And Apostolic Church.
    In thee, in thee, revealèd fair,
      I end awhile my search,
    Thee, the One, Holy, Catholic,
      And Apostolic Church !

Commentaries—I

' Fundamenta eius in montibus sanctis.'—Ps. lxxxvii.

Lo, her foundations are within
  The midmost of the holy hills :
Hark the appointed psalms begin,
  And O how each my being fills !

Deep in the spiritual mount
  Have her foundations diggèd been.
Her body in a shining fount
  Uprises from those pits unseen.

How more than Jacob's dwellings doth
  Our Lord the gates of Zion love !
The place of parley and of oath
  In her,—the eyes, and works thereof.

O thou God's city ! what rare things
  Are spoken of thee through the lands !
What poet excellently sings,
  But still the gestures of her hands

He to my mind tells famously,
  And how God's motions in them throng :
Know thyself, O beloved, and be
  Impassioned with so much of song !

(52)

Commentaries—I

I with my fellows think upon
  The harlot and the world-dweller,
Rahab and eke on Babylon;
  For these are called the kin of her.

Though she so high and they so low,
  To gain her soul they do conspire.
Lo ye the Philistines also,
  The Morians, and they of Tyre,

The Gentiles who know rage and scorn
  And walk their undelighted mart;—
It shall be told, he there was born,
  In the mid-Zion of her heart,

Girt by temptations that assail:
  The Lord shall stablish her therefore;
For any peace she shall not fail
  Nor shall be snapped in any war.

When He the people writeth down
  This shall assuredly be writ,
That He was born within this town:
  O Zion, be thou glad of it!

Be glad that Love in thee sprang forth!
  How should he guard thy temper since
But mortally,—in the poor worth
  Of Israel, an elected prince?

Commentaries—1

The singers shall our Lord rehearse,
  The trumpeters and harpers : O
If the least son of English verse
  Might in that great assembly go !

All springs and songs,—of whatso birth,
  Struck out with blows or rushingly
Leaping from this love-seasoned earth,
  All my fresh springs shall be in thee.

Commentaries—II

' Ego mater pulchrae dilectionis, et timoris, et agnitionis, et sanctae spei.'—Ecclesiasticus xxiv. 18.

IF some agnostic mouth deride
  These songs of private Christendom
(Whether declared be or denied
  That public they have being from),
Look thou again for cure thereof
  My heart but up into thy scope,
Who art the mother of fair love,
  Knowledge and fear and holy hope!

Who could thy twinness then deny
  With Her, the sistered yet the sole?
The creed that proves thee true thereby
  Thou show'st, a microcosmic whole!
To like but less conclusion brought
  In thee, O less but like adored,
Behold, the songs the prophets taught
  Define the Mother of the Lord.

Of her all women blest among,
  From whom the fairest Love was born,
Each lyric definition sung
  Also thy commerce does adorn;
Those titles if her Son approve,
  Are they (wherewith our minds may cope)
Also in us not sprung—fair love,
  Knowledge and fear and holy hope?

(55)

Commentaries—II

The ritual of two thousand years
  In thee to sudden truth hath moved :
'None to himself due witness bears',
  Sole by thy word the Word is proved ;
Who now a vaster faith may win,
  Pledged by thy testimonies warm,
A vaster medium,—but therein
  No less identity of form.

The titles of her Son and Her
  From whom the fairest Love was born
With a like truth but lightlier
  Now by thy love and thee are worn
In this our Christendom, whereof
  Content thou still the thoughts that grope,
Being the mother of fair love,
  Knowledge and fear and holy hope.

Commentaries—III

' Divites dimisit inanes.'—S. Luke i. 53.

WHO is this coming,
  Turned from the door,
From the high feast, Love's feast,
  Feast of the poor ?

It is the proud man
  Who cannot buy
Of the new food, Love's food :—
  Sweet, is it I ?

Strong loves had gathered,
  Rich loves had hold,
Of the soul's wealth, Love's wealth,
  Much skiey gold ;

Oft had they eaten,
  Mistress and lord,
Of the white bread, Love's bread,
  At heaven's board.

Rough went poor spirits,
  In lane or mart,
For the good wine, Love's wine,
  Lean at the heart.

(57)

Commentaries—III

Look, how they laboured !
  Harlot and saint,
By a long fast, Love's fast,
  Sickened and faint.

But O thy singing
  Bound all at last
To a strong doom, Love's doom :
  Must I now fast

When loves, who danced, go,
  Proud loves and gay,
From a glad hour, Love's hour,
  Empty away ?

Poor men who trudged it,
  Ravenous, mired,
At a full board, Love's board,
  Sit gay-attired ! . . .

O then be wise, sweet !
  Now let's go bare,
At the poor's feast, Love's feast,
  To have place there.

Commentaries—IV

'Sir, we would see Jesus.'—S. John xii. 21.

WE would see Love! Sweet, have we not desired,
Sought, hungered, thirsted, agonized, aspired,
Met, clasped, refused? and ever more required
This answer at the end? We would see Love!

We would see Love! Must his companions be
The chiefest sharers of felicity?
Some follower hold our life in custody,
Some appetite or law? We would see Love!

We would see Love! Touch and the things of sense,
Our spirits' pupilage, our minds' suspense
Of expectation,—what conjures him thence
Who is so far within? We would see Love!

We would see Love! His face if none draw nigh
Except their whole lives shatter up thereby,
Agree, sweet! let us look on God and die,
Feel him, one shock, and end! We would see Love!

Commentaries—V

'Perfect God, and perfect Man: of a reasonable soul and human flesh subsisting.'—*Creed of S. Athanasius.*

O WHAT religion could I have
But this that honours truly
A poor dishonourable slave,
By it exalted newly?

How to us sourly oft misseemed,
Through anger or derision,
These princely bodies, now redeemed
By loving arts of vision!

Mental obedience did avouch
The spiritual paean:
Who guessed Divinity could couch
In this supposed Augean?

Chaos is brought into accord,
Now, hushed in rosy laughter,
We worship, though a single lord,
In double mode hereafter.

(60)

Commentaries—V

Hands, bound but to a simple pledge,
    Discover new vocation ;
Instincts, our bodies' depths that dredge,
    Grow teachers of salvation.

O who can doubt the perfect Whole
    In his eternal trysting,—
Love, of the reasonable soul
    And human flesh subsisting !

Michaelmas

ADAM and Eve came running
  From Eden, heavy and sad ;
Michael lightened behind them
  With spears a myriad.
    O love that is broken, broken !
      (Sweet, were we running there ?)
    Lift from us, wings of Michael !
    O sword of Michael, spare !

Mary lay in her chamber ;
  John the Apostle by.
Michael lightened before her,
  ' Behold, thine hour is nigh ! '
    O love exalted, exalted !
      (Sweet, did we nurse the Lord ?)
    Gather us, wings of Michael !
    Circle us, Michael's sword !

There was that war in heaven
  Whereto the worlds were caught ;
Michael fought and his angels,
  Also the devil fought.
    O love that is warring, warring !
      (Us too shall that war rend ?)
    Beat for us, wings of Michael !
    Sword of Michael, defend !

Black-Letter Days

Thou know'st, and I, what Gospel times must be
With a celestial festivity
By our converted souls kept annually ;

How now a Christmas, now an Easter, is
Memorially marked to hold Love's bliss,
Though all our days are hallows, and all his !

Yea, and those others, as the Epiphany,
Apostles' days, or what to Her and thee
For honour are prescribed canonically,—

Such we do often reckon up and know ;
But other hours of less observance, O
How often these unwisely we let go !

Such happy dawnings as, with cause enow,
We might to one or to another vow
Of those great lights that shine upon Love's brow.

Confessors, martyrs, doctors, abbesses,
Saints,— ah, let's honour, in the name of these,
August intentions, sacred memories,

Fine difficulties, new communions ; all
That—Love a little being put back—we call
His aids, his friends ambassadorial !

Black-Letter Days

As, to count up some few and seal them ours,
Lo ! the land's patron, coming with his powers
Of daffodils and all the early flowers

Makes England Love's and our love England's, swears
His happy lovers to a life of cares
That all loves else should freely move as theirs.

Lo, that glad day when under a spring sun
God's loveliest names of Love and Christ are one,
And the young Church's new tradition

Does to the ear of all sweet loves incline
With marvellous prophecy how priests resign
Their office to thy sole hands, Valentine !

But what of penance shall thy Day inflict,
O Love's Contemplative, in order strict
Of rule and meditation, Benedict,

Whose name is, for all hours of solitude,
Love's fasting-days and vigils, in dark-hued
Raiment of sorrows woven by grace indued.

Nor lacks there high Augustine, with those three
His equals, Jerome, Ambrose, Gregory,
Saints, learnèd masters in theology,

Love's divine science and the fount of song ;
To whom the Angelic Doctor does belong,
Dante, and names than his alone less strong ;

Black-Letter Days

(For with love's lore what but love's song entwines?
Rhyme falls not below learning, nor less shines
Cecilia's festival than Catherine's!)

All who to men in scripture or in speech
Reveal this Word of Love, translate or teach,
Still pointing marvels past our present reach.

But O to sing what hot desires have been
To bright zeal at Love's feet converted clean
As on thy feast-day, glorious Magdalene!

Yea, all that racked us since in one consent
Our young virginities together went,
With Agnes, maid and saint, toward Love's self bent,

Adventuring all we doubted on a day
He should on us, as once on Alban, lay,
Who should our selfhoods mystically slay.

Which, if it chance before our deaths or then,
He from our earth's tombs or some worser den
Pluck us, to walk amid his gallant men,

Is brought, sweet, but to pass by only thee;
Wherefore let thine own dawn-star beauteously
Rise again on a new Nativity,

Love's mother for us and God's mother for all
Holding in common their birth-festival.
Nor from this choir let Love's just Name-day fall,

Black-Letter Days

Crowned with that subtle and triumphal word
Pagans and Paynims mazedly have heard,
Which many songs and loves forgot, or erred,

But now return rejoicing whence they trod—
The Name of Jesus !   Ah, Lord Love, Lord God,
From each year's birth to each year's period

Lift us on light wings through these sunny airs,
Till our souls join that flight but Song now shares,
Whose prayer with them invokes for us their prayers !

Churches

WHEREFORE, madonna, should we choose
These excellent rare hours to lose
From play of the delighted sense
Or high enamoured conference
With formal worship to agree
In rites of placid piety?
Churches indeed may serve for whom
No god directly doth assume;
But we—true Israelites!—have found
Worship in our own holy ground,
Wherethrough a grace of doctrine flows
More broad than any priesthood knows:
High as the heaven of our desire
Beyond all teaching we aspire!
Must we remit that wide command
Deep as ourselves,—the while thy hand
(Divine explorer into love!)
Is closeted in a neat glove,
While broideries and ribbons screen
Beauties more duly felt than seen!—
And give ourselves to prayer? our tones
Thank Love, instead of bread, for stones,
Being lost in pomp liturgical;
And O at what rare interval
Do our too-long-beclouded eyes
Rain forth their shining sympathies!

(67)

Churches

Yet we not foolishly expend
These hours, nor to an alien end
Than our linked fingers teach direct
Our spiritual intellect,
Which, though peculiarly it prize
Its own instruction, still descries
All the assemblage here to be
A christened confraternity.
For knowledge, that within our eyes
The manifested god descries,
Teaches that Wonder but to be
A quintessential unity
With all the loves of all men's hearts.
Behold, their dreams, their works, their arts !
Wherewith their visages aglow
Their diverse revelations show,
Till faces seem but veils wherethrough
Love's light hath room to break anew
From the world behind the worlds, and be
Infinite visibility !
How many a love, how many a boon !
One on a hilltop in the noon
Feels him in sunlight ; some belong
To metaphysic or to song,
Meeting through rhyme or argument
That world-encompassing advent,
And feel the intellectual sun ;
One hath a noble friendship ; one
By knife and weight pursues the flight
Of the escaping Infinite.
All, turned from Love's epiphany,
Come to the common liturgy,

Churches

Saluting here, with hymns and prayers,
The Ancient of our days, and theirs.

So to the world our thoughts we bend;
Which here between ourselves attend
A deeper meaning, while abate
Those testimonies passionate
That, in the motion of our blood,
Love's comprehension oft withstood,
And made us foolishly to scant
Our duties; now his covenant,
Largely with us again renewed,
Teaches our pulses, thought-subdued
Throughout this solemn interlude,
After what pilgrimage, how far,
The endings of his courses are;
What End that is, and what the way,
What evils upon wanderers prey;
What Love indeed doth us inspire,
What doth our shrinking bodies fire
Till half a sacrifice and half
A triumph, all a sobbing laugh
Teaches how sacrifice may be
Its own exceeding ecstasy;
How shall achieve the final Deed?
To Christ by this accepted creed,
To God by faith, to Love by sense
Of all our past experience,
By our souls' piercing more and more
Meanings they were created for,
Since first in proud equality,
From treaties and from conquests free,

Churches

Distinct in all this earth of men,
They grew into each other's ken:
Who now, disguised in outward calm,
Mount with the mounting of the psalm :—
' Love drew us from the miry clay,
' Setting our feet upon the way '—
' Within his law is my delight—
' Within his testimonies, bright
' As a lamp to my feet '—' Behold,
' A virgin clad about with gold,
' And raimented in needlework ! '
What marvels in each sentence lurk !
What lights from every verse are shook !
' Lo, Zion ! '—sweet !—' Upon her look,
' The Great King's towers ! better it were
' To be therein a doorkeeper
' Than else in Mesech '—O too high !
Too much of promise we descry;
Thou art but thou and I but I !

But if our thought too easily
Slip from that dear duplicity
Of love and Love, one happiness,
A poorer content to possess ?
If thy tired aspiration stoop,
Lowness by lowness, loop by loop ?
Or if my contemplations fail,
And flutter round a finger-nail,
Or, lighter and more formless, float
Within the laces at thy throat ?
Care not, my sweet ! how often were
Through our encampments earthlier,

(70)

Churches

Our kisses and caresses, known
Love's raids and large invasion !
Upon how many an eve hath he
Confounded our conspiracy
With the vast councils of his joy :
Would soul's or body's bounds destroy
That never temporal circumstance
Should limit his divine advance !
Then, though he be a jealous lord,
Shall he begrudge us, O adored !
These moments from his altar dropped
Or courses of devotion stopped?
Who with a mist did oft confuse
Our sense, and brought it to a muse,
Or, clouding our souls' vision, hath
Lured them into a temporal path ;
Who to a single end doth move,
Convicting so thy heart of love,
Of love my heart,—which still must doubt,
Sweetly perplexed, in church or out,
Whether its assignation be
In thee with him, in him with thee.

The Christian Year

I

Thıs is the hour, foreseen, foreseen of old,
That first in dreams the Angelic Virtue told
To the Bethesda of our blood which slept :
Now the moons wear and promises are kept.
Now strangers' friendship, having run about
The cunning nerves and soul, is all worked out :
Love merely is in either ; whom between,
No whit unreal because all unseen,
Stirs the New-born, the Child brought forth within
This silver-lanterned shelter of our skin,
Where whispers rustle like heaped straw ; our hands,
Serving that Innocence for swaddling-bands,
Clasp the invisible Immanuel thus :
Lo, the Lord's glory is come in to us !
Faint'st thou ? look up, sweet ! can the Mother of Love
Shrink, be perplexèd or afraid thereof ?
Or doubt'st thou if thine honour still shall last
With me, the birth being done and overpast ?
Nay, if I wondered at the first dim sign,
I grow all wonder since thou grow'st all mine !
If first I mused on that which was conceived,
I quite adore since quite I have believed.—
But now awhile soul's rhapsody put by,
And let our thoughts resume their dignity,
Some deputizèd pomp let them put on,
Look, sweet, there shall be visitors anon !

The Christian Year

II

For now the silly senses, one by one,
Do hither from their nightly business run ;
Each crowding churl to view the marvel joins,—
The feet adore ; then hands, arms, lips, heart, loins.
Departing whence, they back to work repair
To find this Advent newly active there,
To learn what worthy company they keep,
Their brutish instincts view as heavenly sheep,
As things celestial their wide-rooting swine,
And tend the copulation of their kine.

Hark, hark ! what questions now in alien tongue
Rumour more conscious servitors along,—
The Gentiles, sweet, becked by thy forehead's star
Which charmed their royal Magians from afar
To this Epiphany ; now, at the gate
While the alert Intelligences wait,
Within, the elect Imaginations kneel :
Lo, the gold circlet of the Commonweal,
For here must Politic his pattern feel ;
Here prostrate falls, with incense for his part,
The half-divine Melchizedek of Art ;
Here brings—but say, Religion, hath thy chest
No jewel nor even simple gold possest ?
Hast thou no gladness in thy mysteries,
Nor odour of admirèd promises ?
Or of what doom then art thou minister,
That thou for gift shouldst proffer dreadful myrrh ?
That thou, where for awhile the world's aches cease,
Shouldst bring no pleasure and shouldst cry no peace ?

The Christian Year

III

Up, up! he prophesied a thing too true!
Up, sweet, and quickly after them pursue!
Care not for martyrdoms thou leav'st behind!
Take sager refuge in the Egyptian mind,
Whose Pharaoh, though his ritual kneel to powers
(Fame, Science, Wealth) alien to birth of ours,
May keep the Child safe against bloody storm:
High Reason in his holy place of form
Decrees security from raging bands
The Herod of this world's Judaea commands;
Who, the great lord of change, our sensual coast
Still ravages with armed and impious host.
How many a virtue and delight must die!
How many a faith and generosity!
How many a sweetness will his rage condemn
If he by chance may slaughter Love with them!
We, while such Innocents his lusts destroy,
Certain of our intent, adore the Boy!

IV

But now returned, Jew not Egyptian,
He seeks retirement where to grow a man.
Behold, thy body's Galilee! thine eyes
A Nazareth none after may despise!
And there he dwells, upon those temples plays,
Or rests from racing in thy fingers' maze
Between those breasts, and still in clasp or kiss
Grows to the after manhood which is his.

(74)

The Christian Year

Whence comes it that some later shall declare
They saw the parentage whereto he's heir,
Saying, 'His mother (this fair face) we knew ;
His brethren, work, sleep, drink, and others, too !'
Or else, 'Can soul's good out of body come?'
But how should all such simpletons be dumb,
If they might guess his Bethlehem of birth
Or feel the heavens wherein he dawned on earth !

But now the world is ware of him ; he goes,
Conforming soberly to all due shows,
'Mid strangers, nor does any more affect
Only the obscure hearts of his elect :
Public profession, vows, the ring, we twain
A single household—so, he lives again
His first presenting and his Temple stay,
The three years following his baptismal-day :
But now more closely (since he earlier trod,
Uttered, was handled, the explicit God !)
In lanes or chambers is his gospel shown ;
The propagation's left unto his own.
Assume the message and the creed acclaim :
The lands' salvation hidden in the Name
Which for his pilgrimage in time now hath
Our bodies' hallowed region for his path,
We his Capernaum, his Bethany,—
But ah ! we too his Mount, his Calvary !

V

O did we think them done or quite forget
The myrrh-king's gift, religious Simeon's threat,
Who cried, 'Did Love of old to slaughter go?
A sword shall pierce through your own hearts also !'

The Christian Year

In mortal pains a more than mortal loss,
Shaped in thy body's fashion of a cross,
Leaves me in vain to seek some ancient grace
Within the changèd purlieus of thy face.
Still from our lips ascends the questioning cry,
And still the voices of the Faith reply:
'Did all those Innocents die then in vain?'
'Not for their deaths did Love on earth remain!'
'Surely his death had end when once he died?'
'Always, in all men, is he crucified!'
'Of old he rose: shall he not rise in us?'
'Even ease affliction by believing thus.'
'Loquacious, violent, unstable, proud,
Who thus about the awful Passion crowd?'
'Who but your own accustomed selves, avowed?'
'The light our faces flung hath strangely failed!'
'And once the sun within the heaven was veiled.'
'Shrinking and a strong shudder taketh me!'
'An earthquake shook the hillock and the tree.'
'Estrangèd grow our hearts; cold, cold our will.'
'Arimathean Joseph felt that chill.'

VI

Bring us, O John his lover, home at last:
Time yet must be, and we fulfil our past.
Us to thy guardianship he hath decreed,
True friend, Morality; grant thou at need
Roof of thy teaching, platter of thy meat,
Who wert with Love of old time wont to eat.
A heavy pathway we till death shall tread,
Mystic survivors of the mystic Dead.

The Christian Year

VII

While it was dark we rose, we came, we saw :
While the Apostles of the moral law,
While the disciples of the reason slept,
Our souls that had through their dark Sabbath wept,
Came with the sorrowful spices of their calm
His dearest memory dearly to embalm.
Yet ere they looked they heard the marvel wrought—
And scattered lie the unguents which they brought—
'All hail !'   Thereon he at Emmaus taught
Our plodding minds and of a sudden where
The doubting senses gathered, he was there.
What loveliness these knew of breast and brow
Is all transfigured and transcended now :
Love's beauty sacred once they did profess,
But O how beauteous is his blessedness !
First eats he with them ; later, at their wish,
Himself provides the fire and turns the fish.
With mouths and hands yet smelling of that fare,
How should they touch meat any other where !
Too full an advent !   Love, awhile delay !
Or let some Thomas of my nature stay
To feel salvation and thy Deity !
In vain, in vain !   'My Lord and God', cries he.
A hundred, yea, five hundred thoughts and dreams
At once behold the light that from him streams.
Love, in a single cloud of radiant dust,
Love, from this earth's austerity or lust,
Love, from the place of shades doleful and dim,
Love is arisen, and we are risen with him,
With him are risen, who is by us adored,
Our Child, our Son, our Destiny, our Lord !

F

Ascension

THE tides of Christendom begin,
  The years of faith and hope,
A cloud of days receives him in
  As our Lord Love goes up,
Still from disseminating hands
Bestowing blessing on our lands.

We shall not find him here again,
  Who felt his first surprise ;
No loneliness or thrill of pain
  Shall draw him from his skies ;
Nor shall a second Wonder smite
Our eyelids with so much of light.

A cloud of days receives him in,
  God unto God returns ;
To his profoundest origin
  Love manifested yearns.
But now he was ! but now, my Fair,
Flickered his presence in your hair.

O look, look ! ere that presence dies
  The Spirit's flame is here,
Descending in new mysteries
  Ere Christ can disappear,—
In whom all living must be shared
That great Nativity declared.

(78)

Ascension

All things he shall in order due
   Bring to remembrance ; he
Infallibly shall hold us true
   And indefectibly.
Incredible is this to prove ?
Ah, how incredible was Love !

A cloud of days receives him in,
   That Christ of yesterday :
The years of faith and hope begin,
   While we must watch and pray.
Our Church her mission hath received,—
We know in whom we have believed.

Council and law shall hold us fast
   And ritual shall grow stale,
Yet sense of this assurèd past
   Shall mightily prevail,
For in your face the Holy Ghost
Kept—how long since !—his Pentecost ;

When, darkly burning in your cheek,
   The rushing blood rode high,
Yet felt its soul and it too weak
   To bear the same God nigh
Who, on the Apostles being come,
Enlarged them into Christendom.

The Continuing Doctrine

YOU whose wit in mouth or line
Of cheek and temple may define
    An exact morality,
    Or a world's theology
Passionately may divine,

Hath your doctrine so profound
Root, to thrive in bloody ground?
    May it in this waste of war
    Speak and not be shamed therefor?
Fewer teachings here abound!

 Who then but ourselves may know
The beginning of this woe,
    Sloth or wry activity
    To so swift catastrophe
Gay intention bringing low?

' What more faulty mind in kings
Or else high state-craftsmen brings
    Nations to their ending thus,
    O fair lovers, than in us
Wrecks our best imaginings?

' Never malice to us clung
But through bloody heart or lung
    Of our fellows now hath torn,
    Never apathy or scorn
Or hypocrisy of tongue.

The Continuing Doctrine

'Once we took mistrust to fere,
Such love-lackers guilty were
    These great dukes and chancellors,—
    If they seek then from their wars
Place for penitence, 'tis here ;

'Here with us, whose wit in line
Of cheek or temple can divine
    A betrayed morality,
    And a wronged theology
Sorrowfully may define.'

Mater Dei

Who hath heard my title?
  Who hath known my name?
While all loves' recital
  Rumours but my fame,
Mine, when young doves' cooing
  Through the land is heard,
When by my renewing
  All the spring is stirred!

Follow, lovers mortal,
  To the heart of Love,
Where through me the portal
  Fleets the holy Dove,
Where through me the Eternal
  Flashes into times,
And the still Supernal
  Multitudinous chimes.

Love, on journey faring
  Through infinity,
Wrought me for his bearing,
  And the worlds for me.
None but my white sinless
  Virgin arms enmesh
Him, the sole, the kinless,
  Archetypal flesh!

Mater Dei

Lovers all, behold him :
   To one end ye move !
In my arms I fold him,
   Archetypal Love.
Diverse love-ways haunting,
   To one end ye throng,
All your wills a chanting,
   All your blood a song !

Have ye seen the vestal
   Glory, swift and clear,
Where upon the quest all
   Hailed the huntress spear ?
Know your mouths the voicing
   First, of love's delight,
While the eyes rejoicing
   Darken with the night ?

Light of vestals massèd
   In my light arose,
I the unsurpassèd
   Dian of the snows ;
In my arms was nursèd
   Love's too mortal bliss,
I the unprecursèd
   Eve of heavenly kiss !

Lo with me imploring
   All your manhoods rise :
Lo on me adoring
   Flame the God-filled skies !

Mater Dei

Daring all the thunder,
  Mighty, unafraid,
I unite and sunder,
  Mother yet a maid !

Follow, mortal lovers,
  Love through me the gate,
Each whose touch discovers
  Her, immaculate !
Turn, behold, and grasp her,—
  Mighty, unafraid !
See and spring and clasp her,
  The maternal maid !

Quicunque Vult

HE who certainly would be
  Saved from foes that harass,
Sworn to the fraternity
  Of the House of Sarras,

Let him follow, undefiled,
  Catholic and humble,
In the Deity the Child,
  Though his going stumble ;

Feel, whatso creeds through him pass,
  In his heart this arrow :
O beata Trinitas !
  O et Verbum Caro !

The Assumption

WITH arms all bare to household toil
 And a little child in hand,
The Mother of God goes on, goes on,
Beside her Peter, beside her John,
And chanting priest and singing bard,
And Michael the warrior for her guard,
 She walks a fertile land.

She treads the ways of Sarras town
 As Nazareth she trod,
She knows to mend, she knows to cook,
She knows on Lord Jesus' face to look,
Before her feet the high kings ran,
She, the Maid, is the Mother of Man,
 She is the Mother of God.

Sorrow and Labour and Delight
 Go surely up with her.
Softly and gaily she goes on,
As when she did her sandals don,
As when she rinsed the cup and can
For blessèd Joseph, a labouring man,
 And God, a Carpenter.

Christmas

I

FIRE within and fire without,
　　Heart and hearth aflame,
Sing, good fellows, round about :
　　Once the Christ-Child came

On a day to earth, since when
　　(Mary, pray for us !)
All good homes of Christian men
　　Keep their Nowell thus.

Fasts are ended, feasts begin,
　　No good thing shall tire :
Fire without and fire within
　　And the Christ a fire !

II

The Child lies not alone :
His voice, his eyes, his fingers, and his heart
Catch at his mother lest she should depart ;
Who being gone
He should be hungry soon and naked-cold.

Christmas

Saved is he, yea, and shown,—
Both held a secret and professed at large
In this committal for a most dear charge
To her, his throne ;
Upon her breast he threatens and is bold.

O Infancy !—to us
Himself hath he presented in no less
Protection of another's littleness.
He safely thus
Dares, till time strengthen him and he grow old.

Clings the Immanuel still
Unto some mortal office ; he is girt
With use of a familiar soul from hurt,
And holy will :
On human love the new-born Love lays hold.

III

Love hath his evangels
    Of how differing strain :
' Hark, the herald angels ! '
    And ' Here we are again ! '

One song without fail is
    Sung before Christ's mass :
Adeste fideles !
    As the priesthood pass.

Fours on fours that follow
    Startle lane on lane :
' Hullo, hullo,
    Here we are again ! '

(88)

Christmas

Sounds the salutation,
  Mighty and occult,
Of our loves' Salvation,
  Quicunque vult.

In the loud army are
  The same dogmas plain :
' Here we are, here we are,
  Here we are again.'

Freshness winning through all
  Evils that destroy,
Temporal renewal
  Of eternal Joy !

Each in words allotten
  Sings from street or pew
Th' Eternally-Begotten,
  Shouts the Ever-New.

Hark the noise uproarious !
  Hark the Church's strain !
Immanuel victorious
  Is with us again !

IV

Ways are foul in Bethlehem !
  (*Sing Nowell*)
Who is this is born anew ?
' It is I that say to you
" Sell your garment for a sword ",—
  I, the Lord.'

Christmas

Guns are loud by Bethlehem !
  (*Sing Nowell*)
Who is this is born anew ?
' It is I that say to you
" He dies by sword who draws a sword ",—
  I, the Lord.'

Flight and fear in Bethlehem !
  (*Sing Nowell*)
Who is this is born again ?
' It is I whom ye have slain,
In your hearts have put to sword,—
  I, the Lord.'

Bursting shells in Bethlehem !
  (*Sing Nowell*)
Who is this is born to-day ?
' It is I who will repay,
I who bring about reward,
  I, the Lord.'

Bayonets in Bethlehem !
  (*Sing Nowell*)
Child, when have we wounded thee ?
' Brotherhood and liberty
When ye slaying put to sword
  Me, their Lord.'

Children dead in Bethlehem !
  (*Sing Nowell*)
Child, is there no ruth in thee ?
' I avenge me fierily,
I the hunger, I the sword,
  I, the Lord.'

Christmas

Massacre in Bethlehem!
  (*Sing Nowell*)
Child, we thought thee sweet and dear!
' Fear ye this? how shall ye fear
The Lamb's wrath, the final sword
  Of the Lord?'

Mary, pray for Bethlehem!
  (*Sing Nowell*)
Thou whose heart is Paradise,
Intercede, not once nor twice,
With thy child, with thy Adored,
  With the Lord.

The Epiphany

I

It was a king of Negro-land,
  A king of China-town,
And an old prince of Iran,
  Who to the Child kneeled down.

It was a king of blackamoors,
  A king of men slant-eyed,
A lord among sun-worshippers,
  Who at the New-born spied.

It was a king with savage eyes,
  King with a queer pigtail,
King with a high and sunlit brow,
  Who bade the New-born 'Hail!'

Back rode they to one country,
  One spiritual land,
Three kings of my soul's country
  Who touched the New-born's hand.

The Epiphany

II

Three kings rode in to Bethlehem
    From Zion hastily :
When Joseph opened door to them
    They entered in all three.

The Child upon Our Lady's lap
    The kings bowed down before :
To see this wonder, by good hap,
    The slaves thronged at the door.

The first king fell upon his face :
    ' O Child, a sign behold ;
The princes of the Gentile race
    Offer a gift of gold.'
Our Lady shuddered in her place,
    For riches men are sold.

' I wot that when thou goest up
    Unto thy throne of might,
'Tis I shall bear the golden cup,
    And come into thy sight.'

Humbly the second king kneeled down.
    ' O Child, thy dignity
Behold, in frankincense foreshown,
    Take thou this gift from me.'
Our Lady covered with her gown
    Her eyes from perjury.

The Epiphany

' I wot that when with offering
   Thou seest thy Father's face,
'Tis I that shall the censer swing
   In that most holy place.'

The third stood forth and bowed his head.
   ' I bring a gift of myrrh.'
Our Lady crossed herself for dread
   When he looked down on her.
' I bring a gift, O Child,' he said,
   ' Meet for thy sepulchre.

' I wot that when thy lips are dumb
   And men defile thy head,
'Tis I shall wait thee till thou come
   To be among the dead.

' When thou art neither king nor priest,
   Thou shalt be friend to me,
When thou of all slain men art least,
   ' Tis I shall neighbour thee.

' But when thou sway'st thy golden rod
   Or drinkest the new wine,
Or goest in before thy God
   With minstrelsy divine,

' 'Tis I of whom within thy breast
   The hidden pledge shall be,
The prayer wherewith thou art possessed
   Shall be a prayer for me.'

The Epiphany

The Child upon Our Lady's lap
   The kings bowed down before,
To see this wonder, by good hap,
   The slaves thronged at the door.

Three kings rode out from Bethlehem
   To eastward hastily.
Our Lady caught, to save from them,
   The Child upon her knee.

III

King Herod was a wiser king
   Than all the Eastern lords ;
They brought incense, gold, and myrrh,
   He sent swords.

They saw a new prophet born,
   Down their gifts they laid :
In dream King Herod looked on Man,
   And was afraid ;

In dream saw God, a Carpenter,
   Marching with his guild ;
Saw the mighty strikes begin,—
   God's death he willed,

Lest on the oppressor roll
   War through town and shire,
Not with noise or bloody wear
   But with fuel of fire :

The Epiphany

Lest the Christ, the people's Son,
  Without end increase,
On his shoulder government,
  And his name Peace.

King Herod was a wiser king
  Than all our English lords :
They bring Acts of Parliament,
  But he sent swords.

Hot Cross Buns

IT was a modern baker
   Who baked Good Friday buns,—
His mind all modern thoughts received,
In evolution he believed,
Heredity, environment,
And one far-off divine event,
Which though far-off it seemed to shine
Showed not particularly divine;
In Man (but not of flesh and blood)
And in a cosmic brotherhood.
He made his buns for great and small,
Setting the cross upon them all,
And filled his poke with pence therefrom;
But he had forgotten Christendom
   Which was his birth-land once.

It was a modern householder
   Who ate Good Friday buns,—
He from his office stopped away
Because it was Bank Holiday,
But worked at home quite hard instead,
Wrote, smoked, ate, drank, and went to bed,
Discoursing with his wife the while.
He ate the buns, with conscious smile,
And saw the cross upon them set,

Hot Cross Buns

While reading in the day's gazette
To draw his own beliefs therefrom.
But he had forgotten Christendom
   Which was his birth-land once.

It was a modern doubter
   Who broke Good Friday buns,—
He with unpriestly fingers there
Broke them between a jest and prayer
And felt within the rending crumb
Rumours of Tartarus o'ercome,
Torn desolations, broken sins,
And the high world of origins,
Hints, prophecies, and ecstasy :
Half doubted of profanity,
Yet felt religion leap therefrom :
For he remembered Christendom
   Which was his birth-land once.

For God looked out on Christendom
   Before he made the suns,
And down the ages saw it rise
With its huge wars and devilries,
Yet a tradition still how he
Was lifted high and scoffingly,
With nailèd feet and nailèd hands,
To draw up to him all the lands.
He saw men stamp upon their food
The gallows guilty of his blood
And so draw double life therefrom,—
When the Lord looked out to Christendom
   And saw Good Friday buns.

Hot Cross Buns

But when God breaks up Christendom
   And Judgement Day is done,
He shall break it down those cross lines twain
Wherewith his son the world hath sain :
A most sure stamp, a most sure sign,
At the heart of the world (a Heart Divine) !
And Christ us save, for his Name's sake,
On Judgement Day, when God shall break—
And the end of things shall leap therefrom !—
The worlds and the world and Christendom—
   As I break this Hot Cross bun.

At Easter

THE kings and lords took up their swords
   And compassed Me about :
The slaves desired to see My woe,
The freemen mocked My overthrow,
   The women cast Me out.

On Me that hour the cross had power,
   I stretched My hands to Death.
Strong in his ancient pride he came,
And in My arms he heard My name ;
   Man's doom no more he saith.

For now I walk while many talk
   In Babel of hard speech,
At even on the bridge I built,
Whereon of late My blood was spilt
   By all men and for each.

Though creed on creed be raised at need,
   And shattered soon, of right,
Yet still I teach by sure degrees
The rulers of the Pharisees,
   Who come to Me by night.

Though age on age the peoples rage,
   The kings of earth stand up,
Yet still within the upper room
I bless, I break the Bread of doom,
   I bless, I pass the Cup.

At Easter

Though nations be at enmity,
  And battle do not cease,
Neighbour with neighbour be at feud,
Yet still I move in quietude,
  And where I go is peace.

Though earth be still in depth of ill,
  And dream of Me in scorn,
For Me there strive the faint, the dead,
The marshals of My host are led
  By crying babes new-born.

As a clear star the ages are ;
  The night is, and they pass.
But till ye walk and listen here,
Ye are but shaken in their fear,
  As in the wind the grass.

Pentecost

I

WHEN the porter let Me in
  Out there flew a Dove:
Down It vanished through your din,
  The name of It was Love.
O, so softly It would coo,
  So sweet It was to see!
O who hath found My Dove?   O who
  Will bring It back to Me?

Must I go to search again
  Through the weary earth?
It would be frighted at your pain,
  And startled at your mirth.
It flies so quick, 'twould fly right through
  The gates of destiny:
O who hath found My Dove?   O who
  Will bring It back to Me?

It will come at your command,
  Nor doubt nor flutter much:
If you should take It in your hand
  It will not fear your touch.
But they who do It wrong shall rue
  Their shameless cruelty:
O who hath found My Dove?   O who
  Will bring It back to Me?

Pentecost

My Father will come down to him,
  And give him many things;
The Dove will overshadow him
  With beating of Its wings;
And I Myself to him will sue
  For grace of amity.
O who hath found My Dove? O who
  Will bring It back to Me?

II

Why swells the tumult in the hall?
  Why wakes the town so late?
The king's men watch upon the wall,
  The burghers keep the gate.
The Prince hath taken sword in hand
  To guard his crown this night,
The meanest of the beggar-band
  Limps forth to help the fight.
Rumour of that last breathless post
  Runs through the markets wide:
'The Riders of the Holy Ghost
  Ravage the country-side.'

Their names had left our easy lips
  As in some idle tale,
But now from all our blazing ships
  Leap up the fires of bale.
So once the homes of Sodom woke
  To slaughter in the night,
So on Gomorrah's altars broke
  The tempest of their might.

(103)

Pentecost

Sound trumpets through the furthest host !
　No whit the storm abates !
The Riders of the Holy Ghost
　Are shouting at the gates !

The princeliest houses of the town
　Whose very names are strong
Lead forth the liegemen of the crown :
　And what shall do them wrong ?
The Banner of the Clouded Stars
　Upon our walls is set ;
The Standard of the Golden Bars
　With all his peers is met :
These, that we fear and honour most,
　Can take no shame or loss.—
The banner of the Holy Ghost,
　A dove upon a cross !

Must we who overthrew the lands,
　Made desolate the sea,
Against these roving robber bands
　Battle so desperately ?
Kinsmen, we fight we know not what,
　Our hearts are sick with fear,
And still the dawn upriseth not
　To show if help be near.
Now breaks, now flies, the gathered host :
　The royal standard falls :
The Riders of the Holy Ghost
　Have stormed the outer walls !

Pentecost

Now battle from each lane and street
  Bursts on the shrieking town,
And under its pursuing feet
  Our lords are trodden down.
Dead by his house the burgher falls,
  Unsceptred lies the king ;
The Riders fire the city halls,
  And as they slay they sing :
' O fallen is their pride, their boast,
  The city of their love !
Ho, brothers of the Holy Ghost,
  Follow the flying Dove ! '

The Repose of Our Lady

DIRGE

COME, squires, no more your lasses entertain,
But hither, hither ! join our mournful train ;
   O measurably come, with footing sad !
Come musically, fluting a low strain ! . . .

Whom bring ye here with candles, garlands, pall,
And anthems, yet through march funereal
   Notes of an irrepressible jubilee
Break forth and feet to quicker dancing fall ? . . .

Nay, what is here of gladness ? this is one
Without whose blessing streams no more shall run,
   Nor wheat nor poppies flower ; a few men
Perchance shall miserably outstarve the sun.

The peasants and the priests afore go on ;
Lovers—they chief who mourn dear hearts foregone
   Into bleak death—on each side bringing her
To her repose, to her dormition,

Company with old men and women ; here
Farm creatures follow ; the wild fox, the deer,
   Slip from the wood, the snake coils from the hedge,
And flights of thronging birds darken the bier.

The Repose of Our Lady

All things are sorrowful, for all she loved.
All that in earth or air or ocean moved
    She from begetting to begetting blessed,
And still in pairing time their loves approved.

The shepherd saw her when he tuned his pipe,
Or plucked out for Neaera berries ripe
    And swollen nuts ; girls, bearing in brown hands
Well-buckets, passed her, their great prototype.

Old men remember her when they were young
And on a summer's bank with golden tongue
    Wooed growing blushes to a tilted cheek,
Which also now is dust and quite o'ersung.

But in that while ere youth was vanquishèd,
Happy who were beneath her favour wed.
    For ever was their table bountiful
And prosperous, O prosperous, their bed !

To her more made than to Demeter suit ;
In the ploughed field the busy corn struck root
    By her ; with great fish seas grew populous,
And little ponds with stickleback and newt.

Rare lichens loved she and the roughest scrubs,
Banyans, and wood-anemones, and shrubs
    Of prickly thorn ; barnfowl and herd she blessed
With chick and calf, and the wild beast with cubs.

Her left hand scattered snows, her right hand rains ;
When she had bound the earth in frosty pains
    Her low laugh loosened it to Spring ; her aid
Was lent to heap the piled autumnal wains.

The Repose of Our Lady

She was of gods the mother, lips now dumb
Kissed heroes in their childhood ; there are some
   Report that she was Leta, Rhea some
Who now by Death her child is overcome.

Old Saturn had her to his bride, they say,
When the Earth, dancing through its primal May,
   Grew such a singing rapture, all who breathed
Must think that jubilee would last for aye.

But she is dead, O she is dead ! yea, now
Hath Death's hand bruised the temples of her brow !
   Lament, squires and young lasses ! that no year
Shall pass without lament's renewal, vow !

Did we not hear the oracles were fled,
And all the antique gods were perishèd ?
   But their and our Sister and Mother now
Is passed to sleep for ever ! she is dead ! . . .

Why therefore do sad march and looks severe
Break ever to a rapture round the bier ?
   Why from your instruments above your song
Such and more sweeter music do we hear ?

Why doth unlooked-for gladness cheer your rout
If the round world be all given up to drought ? . . .
   O thus it is : a dawn more plentiful
Breaks which her dearth alone hath brought about !

She that had many sons had one son yet
Whose growth above all growths of earth is set,
   Who wrestled in his prime with death and won,
Though with hard breath, bruised ribs, and dropping sweat!

(108)

The Repose of Our Lady

Then the world's tree—while even her voice was mute !—
Felt everlasting ice about its root ;
    Frost was upon the skies ;—till Death, outworn,
Shrank, and our Mother heard the Spring's salute !

She is the mother of flocks and corn heaped high,
She is the mother of all fertility,
    And, O than this more gracious and more dread,
She is the mother of Love that cannot die.

Sunshine her smile, her spread hand rainfall gives :
But on her deep breasts Love that ever lives,
    Refreshing all worlds, making all things new,
Throve, who eternally and ever thrives.

He is come down to meet her,—sing again !—
Love who is all the goodness of the grain,
    Who is in tigers and in lilies born,
And sets his hand with hers to load the wain !

Therefore with praise and gallantry and song,
With dancing and with harping go along !
    Soft music hushed her sleep, let gay prelude
The Voice that shall awaken her ere long !

The Voice that gives Orphean music birth
Through all the universe till trees in mirth
    With very rocks and stones join melody :
Sing, all you little things of heaven and earth !

And ye, Behemoth and Leviathan,
Plunge in gross joy, mimic the laugh of man !—
    The Python-slayer to his Love returns,
Godlier than Helios, goodlier than Pan.

H   (109)

The Repose of Our Lady

But chiefly ye, vestals and lovers, ye,
Surround her in immingled company,
   Ye know her office and her person, how
The Mother of Gods and Mother of Love is she.

Go forward, lovers, happy hand in hand !
Go forward, nearest her, O shining band
   Of virgins ! all, lift radiant eyes to see
How soon at their engagement ye shall stand.

Then, squires, no more your lasses entertain,
But hither, hither, hither, join our train ;
   O measurably come, with footing gay,
Come musically, fluting a glad strain !

The Wars

Now while the air with war is full
From Balsora to Hartlepool,
How should the holy Muses meet,
With outstretched arms and mouths discreet,
Lustrate of brow, robed lucently,
To adore Phoebean deity?

Ah, for no battle's roar withhold
From Pegasus his wheaten gold,
Whose neighings pierce no less than all
This noise of guns heroical,
Who hath through all the earth but one
Rightly-bepraised companion,
That sacred donkey which of yore
More than Phoebean godhead bore!

But since! O what strong lie and cruel
Hath so deceived you to this duel,
You riders upon either steed,
And does by artful toils succeed
To turn your wars from Tyranny?
Why must your policies, O high
Imaginations, leave in dole
The siegèd markets of Mansoul,
While the fierce babes of second birth
Shatter the architectural earth,
And 'gainst their heavenly-mountained clan
Goes up the march republican?

The Wars

Lo, the Republic comes! Lo, she,
One, indivisible, and free,
Who moves within the whole world's brain!
Of these Imaginations twain
She is the elder, nor can err
Her eyes from Sarras' barrier,
Wall, tower, and bastion, seen afar!
What names amid her following are?
Athens who drew the first design
Of war; the marshalled Roman line
That broke not when its empire fell;
Many an Italian citadel
That on the German urged its ban
And Peter grown Caesarean;
France, taught of Rousseau and Voltaire,
In the thin tone of Robespierre
Declaiming, in huge voice and limb
Danton, in all who swore with him:
' The populace of France decree
With all lands struggling to be free
From tyrants, their fraternity ';
Last, the huge mobs of Forty-eight,
Before whose summons at their gate
The high kings fled to any den;
Nor rebel swords have moved since then
(Save where—that one more crown should be!—
Men agonized for Italy),
Till now, when all the world is glad
For falling thrones of Petrograd.

Lo where behind their prophet dumb
The silly peoples thronging come;

The Wars

Gipsies in wondrous doleful plights,
With crazy Molls and Bedlamites,
Drunkards and poets, flocks and herds,
And Francis with his flight of birds,
Anthony's fish, and Peter's cock,
Postulants from the caverned Rock
Of Sarras' building : Christendom
Is with her ragged peoples come,
The wildly sane, the fiercely meek !
O fair Republic, though she speak
Of brotherhood as of a King,
Hast thou against her anything ?—
Whose creeds that mystery profess
Wherein none greater is or less
Than any else, but Deity,
One, indivisible, and free,
Shows—O beyond all hope of man !—
The heavens themselves republican.

But now the last days come ! some few—
With prayer and fasting thereunto,—
Have seized, have ironed, those tyrannies
Which are their great Exemplar's spies
In either camp, mistrust and lies,
Hate, anger, apathy.   To death
While these are ta'en, with joyous breath
The eager nuncios prepare
Alliance, and new plan of war :—
Where who but thou is greatest, France ?
Now, now, the long-desired advance
Begins ; now on the Christian tree
Is nailed the cap of liberty ;

The Wars

The labarum that moves on thine
Without an emperor, Constantine !
Beneath, red-caps and red-hats all
Rush, sans-culotte and cardinal,
On the detected foe ! yea, kings
Who knew their folk's imaginings
Here charge, with such as he who bore
King's wrath, and watched the sacred poor,
O Roman and Utopian More !
Now to the aid of Christendom
The guns of the Republic come,
Unlimbering their batteries
Of human huge equalities !
Now, led with Aquinistic skill,
In gallant charges of free-will,
Centuries off, on one same foe,
The great scholastic riders go !
Now the last charge, by Carnot planned,
Follows the sword in Joan's right hand
On Tyranny's last mortal stand,
Calvin is flung and Caesar down,
The sternest foe of the Free Town,
The Crescent, falls ! the field is won,
The days of Tyranny are done,
His last escaping files give place ;
Trumpets, ho, trumpets ! face to face
With foreheads scarred and bloody feet
The Church and the Republic meet.

Open thy gates, O City ! call
Thy burghers to that festival

The Wars

Mankind hath purposed hold in thee
So long, so long,—which now shall be,
For kin is known at last to kin :
Whose high processions moving in
Ward the divine immortal Youth,
Born of a woman, very sooth
And midmost of this glorious whole
Celestial progress !   O Mansoul,
O Sarras, through long winter numb,
To thee, great city, is he come ;
He enters, through thy roaring gate,
Thy chosen and chief Magistrate ;
While from each roof and arch that spans
His pageant scarred republicans
With sturdy hands and throats outvie
Christendom's shouting loyalty
Of spires and gutters : in each street
Bells, kerchiefs, flowers, and voices greet
The crown returned, the chief of men
Elected, the First Citizen :
The sacred paving feels the advent
Of that desired Prince-President,
In whose eternal ecstasy
Now the Republic, one and free,
And the Faith, free and undefiled,
Are met, are kissed, are reconciled !

The City of Man

How shall we build the city of men,
   Love and our mays and we,
Who are not sons of the bondwomen
   But children of the free?

It shall be free as our mothers are,
   Who seem as Sinai,
Moving their heads in that covenant
   So anciently and high.

Though they be broken of men to-day,
   Bruisèd with toil and pain,
Liberty that is the soul of them
   Shall surely stand again.

They by whom we were brought to be,
   Born to the ways of men,
Walk in our midst, of that free city
   Each a free citizen.

Thus to build up the city of men,
   Love and our mays and we,
Being not sons of the bondwomen
   But children of the free!

The City of Man

It shall be free as our lovers are,
  Holily loved and trod,
They by whom we were brought to be,
  Born to the ways of God.

Little, O little, upon our hearts
  Seemed they within our love,—
O but the mightiness in them hid,
  We were afraid thereof!

Queens, and they rendered themselves to us!—
  O but we knew them then,
Republican in Jerusalem,
  City and citizen.

Thus will we toil at the city of men,
  Whose name is liberty,
Jerusalem, the mother of all,
  That is above and free.

Stand fast, stand fast for Jerusalem,
  Stand fast in liberty :
We are not sons of the bondwomen
  But children of the free !

Ode for Easter Morning

WAKE, wake, my Thought! the year's delight is born;
  Hark, the young loves within the valley sing!
Long since thy peers, the Church, the Earth, this morn
  Were out to hail a gladness named of Spring.
Who shall be earliest there? O happy race,
  Begun in winter of a three-days' gloom
To end beside what doubly-hallowed place
  Of the full garner and the open tomb!
        Up, dear sluggard! blessing trine,
        Religion's and the Earth's and thine,
        Sang my spirit out to play;
        Up, my sweet, keep holiday!

This is thy dawning as all feast-days are,—
  Even that high abstract tide of the Trinity
Our sacred duty with thy health doth share,
  And O how much thine own must Easter be!
Easter, that does our byword quite disprove,
  For in green-sprinkled trees and pricking grain,
In alleluias of men's choric love,
  Christmas in one year is come back again!
        Up, dear sluggard! hath the rhyme
        Caught thee ere thy waking-time?
        The sun is up and out to play;
        Up, my sweet, keep holiday!

Ode for Easter Morning

For since that feast was solemnized and done,
    How hath another Advent supervened
(Darker and doubtfuller than that earlier one),
    When died the Lamb that was at Christmas yeaned !
Yet through that Lent, winter, and burial,
    In each our new appointment did arise
Love, in our senses new-prophetical
    Of mirth this public Easter ratifies !
          From thy bathing turn again ;
          Thou through snow and bleaker rain
          Held'st the promise of this play ;
          Up, my sweet, keep holiday !

Why now amid those brushes pause thy hands ?
    Startles thy heart before the tumult now
Heard from the vast excursion of the lands ?
    O fear not, there is none knows more than thou
'Mong all the prophets and high-priests ; thou know'st
    Thy day to this arisen Love belongs,
And through this open meadow such a boast
    Lifts musically in a myriad songs !
          Brushed and plaited be thy hair
          Quickly as thy caution dare ;
          All the world is out to play,
          Up, my sweet, keep holiday !

Yet serious be our laughter, and thy voice
    Singing, a little meetly tremulous ;
This mirth, wherein more worlds than ours rejoice,
    We are a part of it and it of us !
It is come up with such a mightiness
    What heart can lightly hear, beating at ease,

Ode for Easter Morning

His sons, his fathers, and his fellows, bless
  Our yearly resurrection and increase?
        All the world is lucid green,
        With what large encroachment seen
        On Death's winter! Wilt thou stay?
        Up, my sweet, keep holiday!

Ere the Mass grew, how many a shepherd priest,
  Singing his ritual o'er a pile of sods,
Led forth his migrant people on such feast
  In sacrifices to forgotten gods:
His people, lost long ere thy slumber broke
  To a like knowledge of immortal needs;
Enough if thou with thy great Sister woke,
  That youngest, truest, gladdest of the creeds!
        Up, the Church long since is out,
        And her quick feet go about
        To the tomb! no more delay,
        Up, my sweet, keep holiday!

Thou didst not hear the lions of Cybele
  Roaring their salutation to her Love,
Nor feel the high trees shaking over thee
  When he from death ascended; she above
Bowed down, his Mother and his Paramour,
  Unto that resurrection, while her train
Of Syrian pontiffs sang their tale that hour:
  ' Hail, Attis born! hail, Attis born again!'
        Hear thou only from thy lord
        The new tale of an Adored
        Seen of us in happy play;
        Up, my sweet, keep holiday!

Ode for Easter Morning

Thou didst not hear waking Adonis' name
Shrieked from a whirl of timbrelled ecstasy
As to him his diviner leman came,
Descending with her wanton company;
Nor any voice call: 'Now hath Isis found
Her dead lord's limbs the new rice-stalks among;
Now great Osiris wakens from his swound!'
The gods are born again; the gods are young!
Thou wert sleeping while they passed;
Now thy time is come at last.
Christendom is out to play,
Up, my sweet, keep holiday!

Is it a diverse deity they praise?
Or with translation diverse to each tongue
Hail they one god of rice and corn and maize,
Convents and kisses? Hark, another song
Now with those past processions doth accord;
Those resurrections Easter doth renew!
Who is that God, that lover, that dead lord?
Who is that mother? that belovèd, who?
Still must thou thyself bedeck,
Silver chain about thy neck,
Brooch and clasps? No more delay,
Up, my sweet, keep holiday!

Love is arisen: his Mother greets her Son;
Spring knows itself to be but only He!
The glad Church does with the good tidings run,—
O let me find my upper room in thee,
Thou everlasting Easter! what a stone
Of bare negation hast thou rolled away!

Ode for Easter Morning

Now breaks the Dawn whose twilight thou hast shown !
    True is thy possibility of Day !
        Till thy mouth and hands be kissed,
        Lent within me doth resist
        Songs of Easter ; come away,
        Up, my sweet, keep holiday !

Up, more than our earth feels the arising God !
    Up, more than his own Mother greets the Son !
From his eternal death and period
    Love is eternally anew begun ;
Such wonder of renewal as all lives
    Do now in sod or song or spirit prove,
God in himself eternally contrives,
    And Love is rapt upon the birth of Love !
        Thou, till Love hath kissed thee, be
        Never touched or kissed of me !
        Is it he that makes delay,
        He, that is our holiday ?

This is thy dawning, as all feast-days are ;
    Even that high abstract tide of the Trinity
Doth with thy health our sacred duty share,
    And O how much thine own must Easter be !
Descend, belovèd ; our Delight is born,
    Look, how the bright loves on the hill-top shine ;
The Church, the Earth, were long since out this morn
    To hail the Love that shows to me in thine !
        Now thy dressing time is done,
        Thy adornments all put on ;
        Lace the last shoe ; forth to play,
        Out, my sweet, keep holiday !

Invocation

MARY Mother, Mary Maid,
Let thine eyes watch what is said !
Fault of haste and sin of sloth,
Guard, Immaculate, from both,
Till thou, at the full of time,
Breathe in rhythm, thought, and rhyme,
And art my song's justice, clad
In the sign of Galahad !

Thou, whose watch the line ensures
Of celestial prefectures,
Keep me high in courage ; nor
Lose me, Michael conqueror,
From thy legions' marching, who
Were men's poor souls bound unto,
Since began our Grail-quest toward
The Incarnation of the Lord !

Of which souls do thou, our first
Who the deathly waters pierced,
Leaving friendship none to mean
What thou wert and shouldst have been,
Till all living must look back
Now for ever,—by that lack,
O departed, O divine,
Make my work the closer thine !

Invocation

Chiefly thou, O human soul,
Lend me also thy prayers' dole :
I invoke thee and implore,
Stir the heavens evermore ;
Whatsoever chances come,
Let thy lips be never dumb ;
Howsoever lives be flawed,
Spread thy sacred hands abroad ;
So all life, all song, shall be
One magnificence of thee,
O my light of soul and sod,
Do thou, without period,
Plead for me, my sweet, with God.

Epilogue

MADONNA, though we know not well
If sin shall smite me yet to hell,
　　Or shake even thy high head,
Yet this one thing we know, we know
That that which is shall yet be so,
　　And thence be judgement said.

For God, our Love, whose only Name
Is called eternally I AM,
　　As He in thee shows grace,
Still on thy lips is terror, still
May triumph on me to all ill
　　In thy immortal face.

Infinite space, time infinite,
Too hard temptations for my wit,
　　He narrows into thee ;
O'er whom, by whom, I may prevail ;
From whom, despite whom, if I fail,
　　I lose eternally.

Eternally ! from whom beside
Did God our spirits first divide,
　　Ere yet began the Past ?
Ourselves by separate consent
On separate pilgrimages went,
　　To find ourself at last !

Epilogue

That Love which wrought the Mother-Maid
Yet breathed not till her word was said ;
   Even so Love wrought in this.
Symbol and dogma that sufficed
Dully the story of the Christ
   Grew living in a kiss.

The star that guided kings, the bright
Herald of the Incarnate Light,
   The Fore-runner's menace,
Drew thee and me to me and thee,—
Lo, our Lord Love's dread Infancy
   Lay couched in that embrace !

Thence is thy beauty borrowed, Fair !
Thence shall the judgement glance forth, where,
   O vision of the Son !
Through the Now of eternity
Breaks in the thunder of the Three
   The lightning of the One !

And here the kings of song to Love
Bring gifts that do their pomp behove,
   Frankincense, gold, and myrrh,
But I, poor shepherd of the field,
What gifts have I in hand to yield,
   That shall my name prefer ?

How, though I know him full of grace,
Should I before the God's young face
   Dare kneel or gifts unfurl ?
Only I bring them all to thee
Who still, Adored ! hast need of me,
   Being but a mortal girl !

Epilogue

Still must that daring heart delay
To find in me, in me, the way,
   In me the truth, the life ;
And where alone it hath its peace
Must still invent and still increase
   Its consummating strife.

Bodies and souls the world may smutch,
Our fingers too profanely touch
   These holy things, we know :
Yet not for fear of doom to come
Shall singing mouths of love be dumb,
   Or let their moment go !

Printed in the United States
94079LV00001B/262/A